THE

GUIDE TO ORLANDO

1st edition

Eileen Ogintz

gpp
travel

Guilford, Connecticut

Thanks to Regina Yemma for games and research help, and to Heather Kick for fact-checking.

All the information in this guidebook is subject to change. We recommend that you call ahead to obtain current information before traveling.

To buy books in quantity for corporate use or incentives, call **(800) 962-0973** or e-mail **premiums@GlobePequot.com**.

Editor: Amy Lyons
Project Editor: Lauren Brancato
Layout: Maggie Peterson
Text Design: Sheryl Kober
Illustrations licensed by Shutterstock.com

ISBN 978-0-7627-8131-7

Printed in the United States of America
10 9 8 7 6 5 4 3 2 1

Contents

1

Say Hello to
Orlando!

Welcome to the *Phenomenal* City.

That's what Orlando was once called. The Seminole Indians lived here for thousands of years before settlers arrived, and long before Mickey and Minnie.

In fact, Orlando was first called Jernigan, after Aaron Jernigan, a settler from Georgia. The city's name was changed to Orlando 14 years later. Imagine: Instead of roller coasters, there were cattle grazing and cotton growing. Oranges too.

That's what people did in Orlando until the theme parks arrived. Now, of course, more people work in the tourism industry than in any other occupation here. There are more than 115,000 hotel rooms!

But Orlando is a lot more than Walt Disney World, Universal Orlando, SeaWorld, and LEGOLAND. It's a big city where kids live with their families, go to school, and play soccer and Little League, just like you do.

{ **What's Cool?** Wet 'n Wild has the biggest interactive water play experience in Florida.

There are museums and parks, shopping malls—take your pick of 12!—dozens of golf courses, 800 tennis courts, and plenty of lakes to play in. Even if there weren't any theme parks here, you'd have plenty to do!

DID YOU KNOW?

Orlando now welcomes more visitors each year than any other American city—well over 50 million!

Orlando is the number one family spring break destination.

But of course the theme parks are at least one reason you're in Orlando. The first thing you need to know is there are so many attractions here that you couldn't possibly see them all. In fact, it would take you 67 days to do and see everything!

Check out the Orlando website with your parents: visitorlando.com.

A LOCAL KID SAYS:
"You can't leave Orlando without Mickey Mouse ears!"
—Mary, 13, Orlando

First you have to decide where you are going.

Walt Disney World has four separate theme parks, two water parks, and the ESPN Wide World of Sports Complex where the Atlanta Braves hold spring training. There's minigolf, and Downtown Disney has shops, restaurants, movies, and the biggest Disney store in the world. You might be staying at a Walt Disney World resort—there are more than 20 to choose from, and they've got great pools.

Universal Orlando has two parks (this is where you'll find The Wizarding World of Harry Potter); a huge shopping area that is home to SpongeBob SquarePants and all his friends; three fun hotels; and CityWalk with restaurants, shows, and Hollywood Drive-In Golf with 36 holes.

Nearby, Wet 'n Wild water park has a new interactive family water play area with 15 waterslides and more than 100 soakers, jets, waterfalls, and water cannons—making it the largest water activites center around!

SeaWorld is the place to see alligators, baby dolphins, manatees, turtles, and of course Shamu the killer whale.

DID YOU KNOW?

There was a theme park here long before Walt Disney World. Cypress Gardens Adventure Park opened in 1936. That's where LEGOLAND Florida is today.

You can interact with a dolphin at SeaWorld's Discovery Cove and take your pick of 36 waterslides at SeaWorld's Aquatica water playground.

LEGOLAND Florida has a water park too that's meant for younger kids, and if you like LEGOS, you'll love LEGOLAND with smaller coasters, a DUPLO Village, a gigantic Miniland (check out the Daytona International Speedway made out of LEGOS), and an Imagination Zone where you and your parents can make your own creations.

And that's not even counting all of the other attractions like airboat rides, horseback riding, shopping, fishing . . .

There's so much to do, it's smart if you and your family decide on your "must-sees" before you arrive in Orlando. It helps if you take a virtual tour of the parks' websites.

Remember, everybody gets at least one of their picks each day!

Got comfy shoes? They are a must. Sunscreen too! Now go have some fun!

5

Orlando Museums & More!

In case the weather is bad or you're on theme park overload, stop in at one of Orlando's terrific museums:

Audubon of Florida's Center for Birds of Prey: See a bald eagle here! (1101 Audubon Way, Maitland, FL 32751; 407-644-0190; audubonofflorida.org)

The Central Florida Zoo & Botanical Gardens: About a half hour from Orlando. Check out the chance for an elephant encounter on weekends, the bird shows, and bug encounters where you get to quiz the staff. It's smaller but a lot cheaper than Busch Gardens! (3755 NW Highway 17-92, Sanford, FL 32771; 407-323-4450; centralfloridazoo.org)

Mennello Museum of American Art: Really cool sculptures in the sculpture garden around the lake! They're big, made of all kinds of materials, and in some cases, brightly colored. Check out the *Sunbather* by Paul Marco (what a funny face!) and his *Give My Regards to Broadway* with the top hats. You'll also like the giant *Red Dog* by Dale Rogers (900 E. Princeton St., Orlando, FL 32803; 407-246-4278; mennellomuseum.com)

Orange County Regional History Center: Travel back in time to when Native Americans and then homesteaders lived here and see what their lives were like. (65 E. Central Blvd., Orlando, FL 32801; 407-836-8500 or 800-965-2030; the historycenter.org)

Orlando Museum of Art: Special family-friendly guides are available at the museum to help you understand what you're seeing when visiting the "Of Cloth & Culture" exhibition, the "Aztec to Zapotec" exhibition, and viewing American portraits. There are also scheduled drop-in classes for budding artists and special tours for those with special challenges! (2416 N. Mills Ave., Orlando, FL 32803; 407-896-4231; omart.org)

Orlando Science Center: Kids Town is built just for you (if you're under 48 inches tall!). In this mini town you can pick oranges at the Orange Grove Factory, explore what's under a city street, play with boats at the waterfall, construct a dam at the water table, and pretend to be a mechanic in the Super Service Center. (777 E. Princeton St., Orlando, FL 32803; 407-514-2000 or 888-OSC-4FUN; osc.org)

WonderWorks Orlando:
When you enter the building, everything will be upside-down, so in order to participate in the fun, you must be inverted. Step inside the inversion tunnel. (9067 International Dr., Orlando, FL 32819; 407-351-8800; wonderworksonline.com)

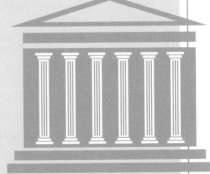

Ready to Splurge?

Whether you want to get a peek behind the scenes at a theme park, get up close to animals, skip the lines at the most popular attractions, or be pampered at a spa, Orlando makes it possible. Here's how:

- You can go to a spa. The Ritz-Carlton, 407-393-4200, is among those in town that have junior spa treatments.

- You can sign up for a behind-the-scenes tour at SeaWorld and get up close with penguins, sea lions, or dolphins. You can even get in the water with beluga whales and sharks with the Animal Connection program. (seaworld.com)

- There are special behind the scenes tours at Walt Disney World too (your parents need to call 407-WDW-TOUR or 407-939-8687 to book). Take a Backstage Safari at Animal Kingdom and learn about how the animals are cared for. Get closer to the greenhouses and fish farm that are part of the Land pavilion at Epcot with Behind the Seeds. Take part in a scavenger hunt quest to save the Magic Kingdom on Disney's Family Magic Tour. Get in the water with ocean life in The Seas with Nemo & Friends pavilion.

- At Universal Studios, you can tour with a guide who can tell you fun facts all along the way—and let you cut in all of the lines! (universal orlando.com)

A VISITING KID SAYS:
"When you meet the characters at the different parks, make sure to have your autograph book and camera ready."
—Hannah, 12, Chicago, IL

TELL THE ADULTS:

- Visit Orlando offers the Orlando Preferred Visitor Magicard, a year-round money-saving discount card that can save you up to $1,000. Download it at visitorlando.com/magicard.

- You can jump in a lake when you're tired of theme parks. Orlando has 2,000 where you can swim, fish, boat, and water-ski.

{ **What's Cool?** Orlando has nearly 100 attractions with new ones being added all the time.

DID YOU KNOW?

Orlando was named after Orlando Reeves, a soldier for a scouting party who saved his comrades.

A LOCAL KID SAYS:
"SAK Comedy Club (sak.com) is my fave thing to do in Orlando outside of the theme parks."
—Lizzy, 14, Orlando

CHECKLIST OF WHAT YOU SEE IN ORLANDO:

- ☐ A giant sculpture made out of LEGOS
- ☐ A sea turtle
- ☐ Chip and Dale (the chipmunks)
- ☐ A magic wand
- ☐ An upside-down roller coaster
- ☐ A haunted house
- ☐ Cinderella
- ☐ A giant piece of cotton candy
- ☐ A dragon
- ☐ Shamu
- ☐ The Incredible Hulk
- ☐ A pirate
- ☐ A giraffe
- ☐ A spaceship
- ☐ Mickey Mouse
- ☐ Mt. Everest
- ☐ Nemo!

This is what I am the most excited to see:

_____!

2

Magic Kingdom

Where's Mickey Mouse?

Sure you'll see him and Minnie at the Town Square Theater, but it's fun to look for the Hidden Mickeys all over the Magic Kingdom—everywhere from the Haunted Mansion (a hint: check out the bottom of the banquet table!) to "it's a small world" (look in the leaves on the ceiling of the Africa room!).

Chances are the Magic Kingdom is where you're going to go first at Walt Disney World. It's the most famous park and where you'll find the Cinderella Castle, Space Mountain, and the Pirates of the Caribbean. There's so much to see and do here, it's smart if you help your parents plan what you want to do first. Take a virtual tour at disneyworld.com and explore the park in 3-D.

There are six different "lands" to visit: **Main Street, U.S.A.** (wait till the end of the day to shop—the stores stay open here after the park closes) where you can grab a cookie and hop on the Walt Disney World Railroad or take a horse-drawn trolley or an old-fashioned car.

DID YOU KNOW?

Mickey Mouse was almost named Mortimer!

Nearly 60,000 people work at Walt Disney World.

{ What's Cool? A Disney employee is called a cast member; those who design all of the fun attractions are imagineers.

You'll probably head to **Fantasyland** first. You've got to stop to take a picture in front of the Cinderella Castle. Your parents will love the rides here because they'll remember some of them from when they were kids—like Dumbo The Flying Elephant, Mad Tea Party (some kids get dizzy as the giant teacups spin), Peter Pan's Flight, and The Many Adventures of Winnie the Pooh.

Little kids and princess lovers especially like Fantasyland, especially now that it is being expanded with the new Journey of the Little Mermaid and the Beast's Castle. You can visit Belle's Cottage too and the Barnstormer Coaster. Don't miss *Mickey's PhilharMagic* 3-D movie.

A VISITING KID SAYS:
"I paid for my own princess makeover at the Bibbidi Bobbidi Boutique. I love princesses!"
—Bronlyn, 10, McDonough, GA

DID YOU KNOW?
There are 11 Disney princesses. Snow White was the first. She made her debut 75 years ago in *Snow White and the Seven Dwarfs*. Cinderella was the second.

Adventureland is where you'll find the Jungle Cruise, Pirates of the Caribbean (take Captain Jack Sparrow's Pirate Tutorial and become an honorary pirate!), and Swiss Family Robinson Treehouse. Kids love the Jungle Cruise because you get to see zebras, lions, headhunters, and elephants taking a bath—all in 10 minutes. Of course, they are all Audio-Animatronics. That means they're life-size robots that seem real. (Get to the Jungle Cruise early! It's one of the most popular attractions.) Kids also love the Magic Carpets of Aladdin, because you can control your own carpet! The Swiss Family Treehouse is about what happens when a family gets stranded on an island and builds the most amazing treehouse in the world. This tree isn't real, though. It's got concrete roots and hundreds of thousands of plastic leaves!

A LOCAL KID SAYS:
"Eat a Mickey ice cream bar!"
—Leah, 13, Orlando

DID YOU KNOW?
The Pirates of the Caribbean movies were based on the Disney attraction, not the other way around.

Like birds? You'll love the Enchanted Tiki Room where the flowers sing along with the birds.

If you haven't ridden a big roller coaster yet, Big Thunder Mountain Railroad at **Frontierland** is a good bet. Each time you ride it, you'll see something different—even a guy in a bathtub! Splash Mountain is here too. They're two of the best coasters in the Magic Kingdom. (Just be ready to get wet at Splash Mountain!)

Kids love Tom Sawyer Island (you can only get here by raft!). Tom Sawyer was a character created by the famous writer Mark Twain. This is a fun place to run around—with bridges to bounce on and caves to explore.

What's Cool? The experts say to make your score higher at Buzz Lightyear's Space Ranger Spin, keep the trigger down all the time and aim for the targets farthest away. They've got the most points!

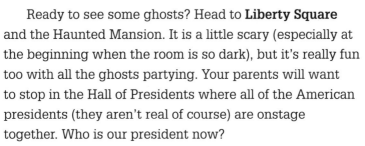

Ready to see some ghosts? Head to **Liberty Square** and the Haunted Mansion. It is a little scary (especially at the beginning when the room is so dark), but it's really fun too with all the ghosts partying. Your parents will want to stop in the Hall of Presidents where all of the American presidents (they aren't real of course) are onstage together. Who is our president now?

If you are ready to sit down, take the *Liberty Belle Riverboat*.

Now if you're yearning for another big coaster, head to **Tomorrowland** and Space Mountain where you rocket through outer space—in the dark. The rockets only go about 28 miles per hour—a lot slower than your parents do on the highway—but it feels a lot faster.

No worries if you don't like scary rides. A lot of kids don't. Check out Buzz Lightyear's Space Ranger Spin where you're part of Buzz Lightyear's command. Did we mention that everyone in this attraction is a toy—that includes you and your parents? You'll also love the Monsters, Inc. Laugh Floor where you can meet your favorite characters from the movie.

Are you 54 inches tall? Then you can drive a car around the racetrack at the Tomorrowland Speedway or fly though space on the Astro Orbiter.

And that's not counting the shows and other entertainment—the Main Street Electrical Parade, the fireworks, and the afternoon parades with the Disney characters (they may ask you to dance with them when they come by).

Keep your autograph book handy!

Staying Safe

- Walt Disney World is a big place. Decide on a meeting place just in case some of you get separated. Have your parents write down the name of your hotel, the phone number, and their cell phone numbers in case you get separated. (Sure, you know their cell number, but in case you forget.) If you do get separated from your parents, look for someone in a Walt Disney World uniform. They can help you find your family!

- Put your name and contact numbers on your cameras and backpacks. Disney does a great job returning lost items.

- Don't try to stand on your tippy toes to meet the height requirements of a ride. The limits are there for a reason—to keep you safe!

TELL THE ADULTS:

- If there are two performances of the nightly parade, the experts say the later one won't be as crowded.

- Mickey and Minnie meet visitors at the Main Street Theater all day. Good chance you'll find Buzz Lightyear and Stitch in Tomorrowland and Woody, Jessie, and Bullseye in Frontierland. But we think it's worth booking a character meal so that your favorite characters come to you and pose for photos while you eat. (Make reservations at 407-WDW-DINE or 407-439-3463.)

- If anyone in your family has special needs, Walt Disney World has a special Guide Map for Guests with Disabilities, special handheld devices that verbally describe each park for those with problems seeing, assistive-listening devices for those with hearing loss, and special accommodations for those with autism and other challenges. Call (407) 824-4321 or visit disneyworld.go.com/guests-with-disabilities to find out more.

- If you stay at a Walt Disney World resort, you get complimentary transportation around the huge resort.

FASTPASS

Want to skip the lines? So does everyone else. That's why Walt Disney World created FASTPASS for its most popular attractions. Here's how it works. You go to the FASTPASS machine at the entrance to the attractions and put in your park ticket. You'll get another ticket with the time you should return when you can pretty much walk right in. While you're waiting, you can head to other attractions that don't have long lines, like Walt Disney World Railroad, "it's a small world," or Tom Sawyer Island. Eat or shop while you're waiting instead of standing in a line. Just remember you can't get a FASTPASS for another attraction for a few hours (read the fine print on your ticket!). And make sure you get the FASTPASS for the attractions you most want to see early in the day because the numbers are limited and they will run out on busy days. Space Mountain, Splash Mountain, Big Thunder Mountain Railroad, and Buzz Lightyear's Space Ranger Spin are among those in the Magic Kingdom that have FASTPASS. You can see all the FASTPASS attractions on your park map.

DID YOU KNOW?

Main Street, U.S.A. is partly based on Marceline, Missouri, where Walt Disney grew up.

Who Was Walt Disney?

When Walt was a kid, he thought the clouds looked like animals. He grew up to be a talented cartoonist, and in 1928—more than 80 years ago—he created a cartoon mouse. His first movie was a black-and-white cartoon (no color in those days) called *Steamboat Willie,* and it was a huge success. He went on to make other famous animated movies. But Walt Disney had a problem. He'd take his daughters to amusement parks but couldn't find enough rides where he could have fun too. So he decided to build a park where grown-ups could enjoy themselves along with their kids. Disneyland opened in Anaheim, California, in 1955, and so many families loved it, he decided to build an even bigger park—Walt Disney World in Orlando. He died before Disney World opened in 1971, but his brother Roy and all of the very talented people who worked for him made sure the Florida park was the way he would have wanted. You can learn more about Walt Disney's dream in a theater near the Pixar Place at Disney's Hollywood Studios.

A VISITING KID SAYS:
"At Disney World you can dress up like a princess all day!"
—Marlee, 4, Connecticut

Princess Power!

The Magic Kingdom is where many of the Disney princesses live, and you can become one yourself (or a "cool dude" prince) at the **Bibbidi Bobbidi Boutique** inside the Cinderella Castle with sparkles in your hair, tiaras, wands, and dresses. (Of course, this costs extra and you need reservations. Call 407-WDW-STYLE.) The Castle Couture shop sells everything princess, and you can get your picture taken here too. You'll see lots of little girls in the park in their favorite princess's dress—Cinderella, Snow White, Belle, Jasmine, Mulan, Pocahontas, Tiana, Ariel, Aurora, Merida, or Rapunzel. Who is your favorite princess?

If you are a princess fan, you'll be happy to know that Fantasyland is getting much bigger with a **Princess Fairytale Hall** where you can meet your favorite Disney princesses all day long and see a new *Under the Sea: Journey of The Little Mermaid*. There are new rides too and even the Beast's Castle.

If you want to eat with your favorite princesses, you have plenty of choices—including **Cinderella's Royal Table,** though that may be the hardest reservation to get in Disney World. It's easier to get a reservation in Epcot at the **Akershus Royal Banquet Hall,** where the princesses are there to greet you too. (For reservations call 407-WDW-DINE.)

Disney's Grand Floridian Resort has a **My Disney Girl's Perfectly Princess** tea too! (disneyworld.disney.go.com/dining/perfectly-princess-tea-party)

MAGIC KINGDOM CROSSWORD PUZZLE

The answers to this crossword puzzle are all mentioned in this chapter.

Across

1) The name of the first Disney princess.
2) This is the name of Walt Disney World's first roller coaster, built in 1975.
3) The state where Walt Disney grew up.
4) The special type of ticket that you can get to skip long lines.
5) This is what people who design all of the fun attractions at Disney World are called.

Down

1) The family that built one of the most amazing tree-houses in the world, found in Magic Kingdom.
6) The land of Magic Kingdom where you will find Space Mountain.
7) The land where you can ride Pirates of the Caribbean.
8) The area in Fantasyland where you can meet all of your favorite princesses.
9) The house where you can see ghosts partying.

See page 129 for the answers!

3
Epcot

Welcome to a place where you can hang glide over California,

talk to an animated turtle, blast off to Mars, or race down a test track.

Welcome to Epcot. This is not only a place to have fun, but also a place to learn. Who knew finding out things could be so much fun? The park is divided into **Future World** and **World Showcase.**

You'll probably go to Future World first. Check out the giant silver sphere when you enter. The Spaceship Earth ride is inside.

{ **What's Cool?** You can design your own coaster and ride it at Innoventions at Epcot. And the website innoventions.disney.com gives you the chance to play interactive games at home based on some of the exhibits here.

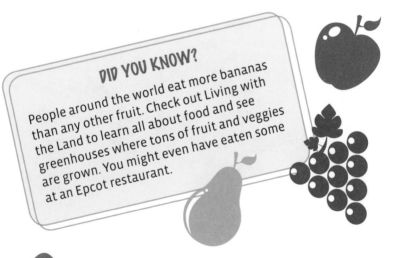

DID YOU KNOW?

People around the world eat more bananas than any other fruit. Check out Living with the Land to learn all about food and see greenhouses where tons of fruit and veggies are grown. You might even have eaten some at an Epcot restaurant.

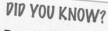
Soarin' is one of the most popular rides in all of Walt Disney World, and it's easy to see why. You'll really feel like you are hang gliding above California over the Golden Gate Bridge, the waterfalls of Yosemite, and the orange groves. Definitely get a FASTPASS for this attraction as soon as you get to Epcot.

Test Track is another really popular ride, but you've got to like fast coasters to enjoy this one (and you've got to be at least 40 inches tall). This is one of the fastest rides in all of the parks as you see how new cars are tested for safety all the while racing around curves and bouncing and bumping on streets.

If you want to see if you've got the "right stuff" to be an astronaut (and you are 44 inches tall), head to **Mission: SPACE**.

A LOCAL KID SAYS:
"I always have water, snacks, and a jacket in my backpack at a theme park."
—Joseph, 11, Orlando

Depending on where you sit, you can be the commander, engineer, pilot, or navigator. But if spinning makes you sick (there's a lot of that in space!), don't go on the Orange trip and opt for the Green Team instead.

A lot of kids really like **The Seas with Nemo & Friends** with more than 2,000 sea critters. Take a ride in the clam-mobile, learn about sharks at Bruce's Shark World, and most important, go to Talk Turtle with Crush. He may be a cartoon character, but he can have a conversation with you. That's Disney magic.

You'll see other kinds of magic as well—and maybe make it happen yourself—at **Innoventions.** This is all about hands-on fun as you become a firefighter or even get inside a video game. Did you know there is a lot of math involved in building a roller coaster? Take a shot at constructing one yourself at The Sum of All Thrills.

> A LOCAL KID SAYS:
> "The World Showcase is my favorite at Epcot."
> —Milica, 13, Orlando

{ What's Cool? There's a talking garbage can in Epcot— at the Electric Umbrella Restaurant.

Kids also love the **Imagination! Pavilion**—from the musical 3-D movie *Captain EO* starring Michael Jackson to the Leap Frog Fountains (the jumping water is a great way to cool off on a hot day) to Image Works where you can make your own music at the electric philharmonic. There's even an Imagination Institute.

Ready to time travel? Check out **Ellen's Energy Adventure** (inside the Universe of Energy pavilion) where you go back to dinosaur times and see where the energy sources we use today come from.

A VISITING KID SAYS:
"Soarin' was so cool. You really feel like you are flying in a hang glider in the sky."
—Dylan, 11, Columbus, OH

Trying all those rides probably worked up an appetite. It's time to head over the World Showcase where you can take your pick of food from around the world.

The **Akershus Royal Banquet Hall** is a good place for a meal with the Disney princesses! But you can also have French pastries, German sausages, pasta and pizza, tacos and guacamole . . . egg rolls, sushi . . . and the list goes on and on.

What's your pick?

- Epcot is a great place for a sit-down meal and offers more choices than just fast food at the World Showcase restaurants. Here's your chance to try German, French, Mexican, and Chinese dishes plus many other cuisines. Kids love the Coral Reef with its huge aquariums. You might see divers feeding the fish! But it's important to make reservations (407-WDW-DINE).

> A VISITING KID SAYS:
> "Test Track wasn't scary at all. It was fast! Get a FASTPASS for Test Track so you don't have to wait."
> —Briana, 11, New Hampshire

- The best place to find characters at Epcot is at Innoventions West.

- Soarin', Test Track, and Mission: SPACE are among the most popular Epcot attractions. Go there first and use FASTPASS. World Showcase is best later in the day. It doesn't even open until 11 a.m.

Pin Mania!

Wherever you go at Walt Disney World, you'll see adults and kids wearing lanyards around their necks that are covered with shiny pins. There are thousands of different ones! (disney store.com) You can buy a pin to commemorate your birthday or your favorite ride, character, or Disney movie. There are light-up pins, pins that spin, and 3-D pins.

The Walt Disney Company has always offered collectible Disney pins. During the Millennium Celebration in 1999, they encouraged guests to trade pins, and today, many grown-ups and kids do at the parks and even on eBay. (At Epcot, Innoventions Plaza is the place to go for pin-trading.)

Want to start trading? Find a Disney pin you like and look for a Disney cast member wearing a green pin lanyard. They can only trade to kids!

A VISITING KID SAYS:
"I love collecting Disney pins. I have over 90 so far!"
—Macy, 10, Connecticut

Ready to Go around the World—
In a Few Hours?

Here's your chance to travel around the world and chat up the locals without even getting on a plane.

Welcome to Epcot's World Showcase. There are Kidcot Fun Stops at each country of World Showcase where you can make a craft.

Check out the totem pole at Canada, the Eiffel Tower at France, and the shops selling Moroccan hats (called fezzes). Taiko drummers are often outside the Japan Pavilion, and you can meet heroes from American history at the American Adventure. Check out the fish in the Chinese koi pond and the three-headed troll at Norway.

The World Showcase is a great place to sample food from different countries, learn some words of a foreign language, see a show, and of course, at night watch the *IllumiNations: Reflections of the Earth* fireworks show that tells the story of the creation of the Earth. You can watch it around the World Showcase Lagoon. It's amazing!

DID YOU KNOW?
Epcot is triple the size of the Magic Kingdom.

{ **What's Cool?** You get free samples of all different kinds of Coca-Cola sodas from around the world at Club Cool in Future World.

LIVING WITH THE LAND

When you visit Epcot, you can visit a place where a whole bunch of food is grown when you take a boat ride at Living with the Land through the rainforest and greenhouses.

There are six plant parts that we eat: roots, stems, leaves, flowers, fruits, and seeds.

Draw a line between each vegetable and its type.

Root	Lettuce
Stem	Tomato
Leaves	Sunflower Seeds
Flower	Asparagus
Fruit	Broccoli
Seed	Carrot

What are the four things that all plants need to survive?

1) _____

2) _____

3) _____

4) _____

See page 129 for the answer key.

4
Animal Kingdom

Ready to talk to the animals?

Disney's Animal Kingdom certainly is the place to do it—starting with tiny bugs.

At the Tree of Life, there's the 3-D movie ***It's Tough to be a Bug!*** hosted by Flik, star of *A Bug's Life*. See how important tiny bugs really are! But if you hate spiders and roaches, you probably want to skip this movie. So will your younger brothers and sisters. Little kids think it's scary.

> A VISITING KID SAYS:
> "I love 'It's Tough to be a Bug.' At the end you'll feel like bugs are walking under you!"
> —Dylan, 7, Connecticut

There are plenty of other things to do here. Check out **DinoLand U.S.A.** Ready to ride a flying triceratops? Walk underneath a giant brachiosaur skeleton and join the dino dig in The Boneyard, make your way through a maze full of fossils, play some carnival games, and if you're ready for a scary ride, time travel back to rescue a 16-foot dino at DINOSAUR. It's fast and dark (and you've got to be 40 inches tall).

Don't miss ***Finding Nemo: The Musical*** (it's at DinoLand's Theater in the Wild).

Ready to go to Africa now? On **Kilimanjaro Safaris,** you'll see hippos, lions, rhinos, and elephants up close! Take a stroll on the **Pangani Forest Exploration Trail** (have you ever seen a naked mole rat?). And say hi to the gorilla family. See the baby?

No plane is needed to visit Asia—just a walk over a bridge. Ready to get wet? **Kali River Rapids** is one of the wettest rides at Walt Disney World. **Expedition Everest** is in Asia too, and it's one of the most popular attractions here (get your FASTPASS early!) and the tallest mountain in Walt Disney World. Go for it if you are 44 inches tall and like dark and wild rides. Ready to meet an abominable snowman?

A LOCAL KID SAYS:
"When it rains at a theme park, get a poncho and go have fun!"
—Madison, 9, Orlando

The **Maharajah Jungle Trek** is a lot calmer. You can walk down this trail and see all kinds of weird and wonderful creatures—colorful birds, tigers, bats, Komodo dragons . . . And then at the *Flights of Wonder* show, see the birds do tricks. It's really fun!

Got your autograph book? **Camp Minnie-Mickey** is where you'll find all of your favorite characters as well as the *Festival of the Lion King* show. (You can sing along with the songs you know!)

There's lots of music throughout Animal Kingdom—African bands perform in the village of Harambe, and there's a jungle parade of Disney characters too.

Find any **Hidden Mickeys** yet?

A LOCAL KID SAYS:
"I look at my Disney pins when I'm waiting in line. Trading pins is my favorite thing to do at the parks."
—Caroline, 10, Orlando

TELL THE ADULTS:

- FASTPASSES for Expedition Everest are often gone before noon. If you want to take in this high-speed train that climbs up snowy peaks (and you are at least 44 inches tall), get your FASTPASS as soon as you get to the park. Ditto for DINOSAUR and Kali River Rapids. The lines for Kilimanjaro Safaris get shorter after lunch. Go then!

- You'll find your favorite Disney characters at the end of short trails at Camp Minnie-Mickey, but be prepared for possibly long lines. Consider having breakfast with Donald Duck, Mickey, Daisy, and Goofy at the Tusker House to get autographs and pictures. If you plan to park-hop, start at Animal Kingdom, the experts say, and get there before the park opens because there's often a musical party first thing in the morning!

> **A LOCAL KID SAYS:**
> "Have a reusable water bottle and Band-Aids in your backpack."
> —Rebecca, 13, Orlando

- Most of the attractions at Disney's Animal Kingdom are outdoors. It can get very hot! Make sure to bring reusable water bottles and get out of the sun when you can.

It Pays to Be Green

Got a reusable water bottle? All of that plastic from disposable water bottles is really bad for the planet. Using a reusable water bottle is one little thing you can do that can have a big impact. And it can become a souvenir when you put stickers from your trip to Orlando all over it!

A visit to Disney's Animal Kingdom can help you understand why it's important to be greener at home and on vacation. A healthier planet means a better environment for all of the animals. Visit Rafiki's Planet Watch—the park's conservation headquarters—to find out how else you can help.

See the interactive video that will tell you about endangered animals, or try out the Animal Cams to watch gorillas, hippos, and other animals. Check out the EcoWeb and link to conservation organizations. Be transported to the rainforest at the 3-D audio Song of the Rainforest. At the same time, meet some animal handlers, see some animals, and visit an animal hospital. Here are some simple things you can do to help the environment at home and on vacation:

- Turn off the lights in your hotel room when you leave.
- Recycle.
- Reuse towels in the hotel.
- Take public transportation when you can.
- Take shorter showers.

What's Cool? You can get up close and personal with all kinds of critters at Animal Kingdom. Look for them with their keepers as they walk around the park!

A VISITING KID SAYS:
"Expedition Everest is my favorite ride at Walt Disney World—especially when you go backwards and down! It is sort of scary but fun."
—Jonathan, 14, Denver, CO

DID YOU KNOW?

The benches here are made from recycled plastic milk jugs.

DID YOU KNOW?

The Tree of Life is 145 feet tall and has carvings of 325 animals. It's a symbol of how life on Earth is all connected. How many different animals can you spot?

Cooling Off

It can get very hot in Orlando in the summer, especially at Disney's Animal Kingdom. Take a break in the hottest part of the day and go back to your hotel for a swim (most hotels have awesome pool complexes including waterslides!) and return in the evening.

Opt for Disney Water Parks. There's Disney's Typhoon Lagoon (the idea is a typhoon hit a tiny resort village but the locals rebuilt their community as a "watertropolis"). There are huge waterslides, Castaway Creek circular river, and Ketchakiddee Creek for kids 4 feet tall and under, complete with slides, waterfalls, and squirting whales. You can snorkel through a coral reef built around a sunken ship.

Disney's Blizzard Beach, another water park, was "created" by a storm that dropped a mountain of snow onto Walt Disney World. The ski runs became waterslides! There's also a Tike's Peak here for younger kids and an 8-lane waterslide that lets you race. Tell your parents that especially on hot days, the water parks get crowded early.

There are other water parks in Orlando too—Wet 'n Wild, a new water park that has just opened at LEGOLAND (legoland.com), and Aquatica at SeaWorld (aquaticabysea world.com)—with raft and tube rides, wave pools, and Kata's Kookaburra Cove for little kids.

Answer the questions and the use the circled letters to spell out the secret word!

1) This reptile is the world's largest lizard, and you will find it in the Maharajah Jungle Trek.

   _ _ _ _ _ _ _ _(_) _ _ _

2) This is the highest mountain in Africa.

   _ _ _ _ (_) _ _ _ _ _ _

3) This is the name of a scientist who studies dinosaurs.

   _ (_) _ _ _ _ _ _ _ _ _ _ _ _

4) Covered in black and white stripes, this animal lives in large herds all around the savannas of Africa.

   (_) _ _ _ _

5) This word means "lion" in Swahili (a language spoken in Africa) and is also the main character of *The Lion King*.

   _ (_) _ _ _

6) A beautiful ocean animal with waving tentacles that Nemo loves to play in.

   _ _ _ _ _ (_) _

7) The kind of bug that Hopper is from *A Bug's Life*.

   (_) _ _ _ _ _ _ _ _ _ _

Secret Word: _ _ _ _ _ _ _

See page 129 for the answers!

5

Disney's
Hollywood Studios

Ready to rock 'n' roll?

The Rock 'n' Roller Coaster Starring Aerosmith
not only goes fast, but it will flip you three times.
(Don't eat before getting on this ride, and you've got
to be 48 inches tall!)

If that weren't scary enough, there's **The
Twilight Zone Tower of Terror** where you
walk through the haunted hotel lobby into
an elevator that plunges, shoots up, and
drops again.

A lot less scary is **The Great Movie
Ride** where you actually drive through
scenes of old movies like *Mary Poppins*,
Alien, and some famous old movies from
before your parents were even born.

{ What's Cool? There are lots of video games at the Pizza Planet Arcade near the *Muppet Vision 3-D* attraction.

DID YOU KNOW?

Mickey Mouse wasn't Walt Disney's first famous
character; Oswald the Lucky Rabbit was. Disney's
Hollywood Studios Resort is a great place to find
out more about Walt Disney, without whom Disney
World wouldn't be here. Check out *Walt Disney:
One Man's Dream* in the theater near Pixar Place.

But even better is to get inside a video game at **Toy Story Mania!** Get on your 3-D glasses and aim your shooter at the targets. The funnest part is your score gets better every time you ride with Woody, Buzz, and pals cheering you on!

Did you know there is a real movie studio here? That's what the **Studio Backlot Tour** will show you—where the movies and TV shows you've seen are made. Check out how fires and battles can seem so real on-screen! Look at all the costumes! Walt Disney World has more costumes

than anyone—2.5 million! Ready for Catastrophe Canyon? Get ready for a flash flood, explosion, fire, and even problems with the road—all part of the Studio Backlot Tour that shows you how special effects are created in movies. If you like movies, stop at the American Film Institute Showcase to see all of the stuff from Hollywood—costumes and props from TV and films. There might be something from a movie you've seen!

A LOCAL KID SAYS:
"Eat at Hollywood & Vine.
It's an old-fashioned diner, and
some of the characters are there
at breakfast and lunch."
—Rebecca, 13, Orlando

Star Tours— The Adventures Continue is another 3-D attraction that takes place on the same kind of flight simulator astronauts and pilots use to train. Do you feel like you're really racing through space? It can be very bumpy, so skip this if you tend to get motion sickness.

At **Sounds Dangerous Starring Drew Carey,** you get special headphones that will provide surround sound. The audience hears and sees all the silly mistakes Drew Carey makes as an undercover detective.

{ What's Cool? If you want to get wet, ride on the left side of the Studio Backlot Tour and get ready for Catastrophe Canyon!

DID YOU KNOW?
Lightning supposedly struck the Hollywood Tower Hotel on Halloween in 1939, hitting a guest wing and an elevator carrying five people. The Twilight Zone Tower of Terror is one of the scariest—and most popular— rides here. If you change your mind at the last minute, there is a special exit.

There's lots of shopping here along **Hollywood Boulevard** and **Sunset Boulevard** (named for Los Angeles streets, of course). If you want to get your face painted, head to **Special FX Make-UP.**

Buy your pins at **Crossroads of the World.** If you've survived the Rock 'n' Roller Coaster, you might want to get something at the **Rock Around the Shop.** If you like villains, don't miss **Villains in Vogue** with souvenirs for all your favorite bad guys—and girls.

When you're ready for a break, head to the **Honey, I Shrunk the Kids Movie Set Adventure.** It's a giant playground with 30-foot pieces of grass, a giant toy truck and spiderwebs, giant tree stumps, and huge LEGO blocks—all designed so you can see the world from a bug's perspective. You can crawl, climb, slide, and get wet too.

Watch out for the leaky hose . . .

{ What's Cool? The 3-D Toy Story Mania! makes you feel like you are inside a giant video game—and the size of a toy!

TELL THE ADULTS:

- Visit Rock 'n' Roller Coaster Starring Aerosmith, Tower of Terror, *Voyage of the Little Mermaid*, and Toy Story Mania! as close to park opening as possible and get FASTPASSES because they often run out on busy days.

- Disney Channel characters hang out in Animation Courtyard, and the *Toy Story* gang on Pixar Place. You'll find Mickey, Donald, Chip, and Dale in front of the big sorcerer's hat. You'll also see characters at the Streets of America.

A LOCAL KID SAYS:
"Talking to people while waiting on line helps make the time go faster."
—Ginny, 13, Orlando

DID YOU KNOW?
Hollywood is the city in California where the movie business got started. Disney's Hollywood Studios has attractions and shows based on everyone's favorite Disney movies like *Toy Story*, *The Little Mermaid*, and the Indiana Jones series.

Autographs & Photos

Keep that autograph book handy! There are plenty of places to meet up with the characters at each of the parks, but sometimes you'll have to wait in line for the opportunity. And sometimes, you get there just as the characters are leaving!

Tell your parents to check that day's guide map to see where your favorite characters will be. Another way to guarantee that you can meet and greet your favorites is to ask your parents to book a character meal. They come around to your table while you are eating to pose for pictures and sign autographs. Meet Handy Manny and Special Agent Oso, plus June and Leo from *Little Einsteins* at Hollywood & Vine. (Call 407-WDW-DINE or go to disneyworld.com/dining to make reservations.)

You can also save time if you book reservations at other fun places to eat here—the '50s Prime Time Café (check out the little black-and-white TVs!) or the Sci-Fi Dine-In Theater where the tables are old-fashioned cars and "stars" twinkle overhead as if you were at an old outdoor drive-in movie.

Some of the restaurants also have a dinner and show combination that includes seating for the popular *Fantasmic!* It's all about planning ahead!

The Show Goes On!

There's entertainment everywhere—mostly with a TV or movie theme—at Disney's Hollywood Studios. It's smart to figure out what times the shows are offered and which ones you really want to see ahead of time. And don't forget to volunteer if you want to be part of the action!

Check out the shows with songs from movies like *High School Musical* and *Camp Rock* in front of the big sorcerer's hat:

- Line up early for *Fantasmic!*, which combines water, lasers, music, and more at night, letting you imagine what Mickey might be dreaming about. (Be sure to line up at least an hour before the show, and if you're near the front, be ready to get wet!) Check to make sure it is going to be offered the night you are visiting the park.

- Pixar Pals Countdown to Fun Parade

- The *Indiana Jones Epic Stunt Spectacular!*, which shows you how special effects are done in the movies (just don't try these stunts at home!)

- The *American Idol Experience*, where three park guests are chosen to sing their hearts out (you have to be 14!)

- *Muppet Vision 3-D* show

- *The Voyage of the Little Mermaid* (check out the screen of water!)

- *Disney Junior—Live on Stage!* is a fave with the littlest kids.

- *Beauty and the Beast—Live on Stage*

See page 130 for the answers!

WORD PUZZLE

Using the key at the bottom, write the letters under the symbols to figure out the secret phrase.

For example: 🚲🏙 🏚✈ = b i r d

_ _ _ _ _ _ _ _ _   _ _ _

_ _ _ _ _ _ _ _   _ _ _ _

_ _ _ _ _ _

a=✔ b=🚲 c=🏙 d=✈ e=🎁

f=🏭 g=🏛 h=🏠 i=🏚 j=✉

k=🦟 l=? m=👤 n=👁 o=🚤

p=🛣 q=⛰ r=🏓 s=✦ t=🚇

u=📣 v=📦 w=⚑ x=🔈 y=♥

z=🦟 .=⬛ !=🚌 ,=🌶

6

Universal Orlando

Can you help get the Statue of Liberty back from the villains

of the Sinister Syndicate?

Sure you can—on **The Amazing Adventures of Spider-Man at Universal Orlando's Islands of Adventure.** Many people think this is the best attraction here. It's a wild ride as you get into the middle of the fight between good and evil!

Universal Orlando has two theme parks: **Islands of Adventure** has seven "islands" (including The Wizarding World of Harry Potter and Seuss Landing), two big coasters, and a **Toon Lagoon** area where you can see the characters. **Universal Studios** is divided into six sections and includes

A VISITING KID SAYS:
"Go to Spiderman first and then The Wizarding World of Harry Potter. I like Spiderman better than the Harry Potter ride."
—Alex, 12, Denver, CO

DID YOU KNOW?

The Amazing Adventures of Spider-Man was the first attraction to combine moving, motion-based platform ride vehicles, 3-D movies, and live action.

the **Hollywood Rip Ride Rockit** (the track's shaped like a treble clef!) and great shows like *Animal Actors on Location* (you might even get to be part of the show!), *Beetlejuice's Graveyard Revue*, and *The Blues Brothers.* If you ever wondered how actors are transformed to look like film monsters, check out the *Horror Make-Up Show*.

There's also a *Fear Factor Live* show with crazy, icky challenges the contestants have to complete. (You can watch but have to be 18 to compete!)

The hardest choice will be deciding which park to visit first! The good news is they are both compact and easy to cover in one day. At Islands of Adventure, you should go to **The Wizarding World of Harry Potter** and The Amazing Adventures of Spider-Man first because that's where the lines will be the longest. If you like fast coasters, you'll also want to visit the **Incredible Hulk Coaster,** but get ready to be shot out like a cannonball and then flung upside down 100 feet above the ground!

{ **What's Cool?** You'll be transformed into a Minion in the new Despicable Me Minion Mayhem attraction at Universal Orlando.

As if that isn't enough, there's **Doctor Doom's Fearfall** where you're rocketed 150 feet up in the air and then dropped faster than gravity itself. If you like getting wet, there's **Dudley Do-Right's Ripsaw Falls**—a flume ride. And also the **Jurassic Park River Adventure** (uh-oh, some of the dinosaurs have escaped!); get ready for a big drop—and to get wet again!

If you want more thrills, join the crowd at Universal Studios' **Hollywood Rip Ride Rockit,** which some say is one of the most technologically advanced coasters in the world. The drop is almost straight down, and there are loops and twists.

> A VISITING KID SAYS:
> "I love The Hulk. It's really fast, and it loops."
> —Michelle, 10, St. Petersburg, FL

DID YOU KNOW?

Universal Orlando actually has two theme parks—Universal Studios and Islands of Adventure. The Wizarding World of Harry Potter is inside Islands of Adventure.

Kids love **The Simpsons Ride** where you visit a theme park thought up by Krusty the Clown. You'll hear a lot of the voices of the actors who have been on the show.

Not scared enough? At **Disaster!** you experience an earthquake, and at **Men in Black Alien Attack** you volunteer as a trainee to stop aliens. Aim for the aliens' eyes in the Men in Black Alien Attack and keep shooting. Other riders may shoot at your vehicle, making your car spin! (This is a really popular ride too, so go early!)

Revenge of the Mummy is a dark, scary ride and a coaster. Think of racing through spooky tombs! Talk about a curse!

You'll be in the middle of a tornado at **Twister,** with special effects from the movie.

DID YOU KNOW?

Dragon Challenge in The Wizarding World of Harry Potter is the highest coaster in the park and has the longest drop—115 feet!

The Wizarding World of Harry Potter

Welcome to Hogsmeade. For those who don't know, that's where Harry Potter and his pals attend wizarding school. You'll feel like you've stepped inside the Harry Potter books or movies. If you haven't seen any of the Harry Potter movies or read the books, you might want to before you visit.

The Wizarding World of Harry Potter is inside Universal's Islands of Adventure, and it can be very crowded—even to get into the shops—so it's smart to get there as soon as the park opens. If that doesn't work, go late in the afternoon because most people come here first.

Ready to fly? Join Harry Potter and his pals on Harry Potter and the Forbidden Journey. It's easy to see why the lines are so long, but half the show happens while you are waiting in line (you'll get on faster if you use the single riders

DID YOU KNOW?

More than three million cups of Butterbeer have been sold at The Wizarding World of Harry Potter. You may know Butterbeer from the Harry Potter movies and books. It tastes kind of like butterscotch and shortbread cookies, and, of course, it's not alcoholic.

line) as you make your way through Hogwarts castle. (Do you see the portraits of the four founders of Hogwarts? Sometimes they come alive!) Where else can you fly over Hogwarts, escape a dragon attack, get up close to the Whomping Willow, and find yourself pulled into a Quidditch match?

There's also the Dragon Challenge—two high-speed coasters, the Chinese Fireball and the Hungarian Horntail. You'll have an entirely different experience on each. The idea is you are getting ready for the first task of the Triwizard Tournament. If you aren't tall enough or don't like scary coasters, try Flight of the Hippogriff instead.

And when you're done, you can buy a Screaming Yo-Yo or Extendable Ears at Zonko's, send a postcard with a Hogsmeade postmark from the Owl Post, or buy a magic wand at Ollivanders (after the wand picks you!). Be prepared that only about 24 people at a time can get into Ollivanders so the wait can be long. You can also buy a Marauder's Map at Filch's Emporium of Confiscated Goods or other magic supplies at Dervish and Banges.

TELL THE ADULTS:

- Guests of each of the three on-site hotels at Universal Orlando—Loews Portofino Bay Hotel, the Hard Rock Hotel, and Loews Royal Pacific Resort—can skip the regular theme park lines at participating rides and attractions just by showing their hotel key card—a benefit worth up to $89 per person, per day! (universalorlando.com/Hotels/Three-World-Class-Hotels.aspx) If you aren't staying on-site, you can buy a Universal Express Plus pass that enables you to bypass the lines. Prices start at $19.99 per person and vary depending on when you visit. (universalorlando.com/Theme-Park-Tickets/Universal-Express/Express-Plus-Passes.aspx)

A VISITING KID SAYS:
"The Blue Man Group is amazing!"
—Keenan, 11, Vermont

- Universal CityWalk runs between the two theme parks, and this is where you can eat—there are more than 20 restaurants—go to the movies, watch street performers, see Blue Man Group in a revamped show (get tickets at universal orlando.com), and shop. You can watch NBA games on 15-foot screens at NBA City.

- Some of the attractions will get you wet. Bring ponchos or rain jackets.

- If you also plan to visit SeaWorld and Wet 'n Wild, there are Orlando Flex Tickets that will save you money. (Undercovertourist.com offers discounted tickets as does mousesavers.com.)

{ What's Cool? Many of the Egyptian hieroglyphics decorating the walls in Revenge of the Mummy spell out real words.

Scary Rides

Are you ready?

Universal Orlando has plenty for younger kids to do but is especially known for its thrilling and fast attractions like Revenge of the Mummy and the Incredible Hulk Coaster.

First, you have to see if you are tall enough. No tiptoes either!

Next, don't make yourself do something you are scared about. That's no fun! Every ride typically has a way to "escape" if you change your mind when you are standing in line.

These rides can be very dark, bumpy, and loud. If you get motion sickness like a lot of kids and grown-ups, you probably want to skip rides that have a lot of sharp curves. Take a virtual tour of the parks beforehand to see what rides you might want to skip this time. There are plenty of other fun attractions!

Remember, a visit to a theme park is supposed to be fun. You don't have to ride any attraction you don't want to! And there's always next time . . .

A LOCAL KID SAYS:
"Revenge of the Mummy is my favorite Universal ride!"
—Alisa, 13, Orlando

Little Park-Goers

Universal Orlando may have some of the best coasters any-where, but it's also got a lot for little park-goers—like Islands of Adventure's Seuss Landing. Here's your chance to eat green eggs and ham and ride through 18 different Cat in the Hat scenes, climb on board the Caro-Seuss-el where you'll find an array of unusual creatures from the imagination of Dr. Seuss, go for a High in the Sky Seuss Trolley Train Ride! or try to avoid water being squirted at you on One Fish, Two Fish, Red Fish, Blue Fish.

Costumed characters including Shrek, Donkey, Sponge-Bob SquarePants, and Woody Woodpecker are easy to find at Universal Studios, and they're happy to pose for pictures and sign autographs.

Check out Camp Jurassic (explore secret caves and wander through a mysterious amber mine) and Me Ship, The Olive, a three-story boat-themed play area where kids can run around and shoot water cannons.

At Universal Studios, there's the show called *A Day in the Park with Barney*, Shrek 4-D, and Woody Woodpecker's Kid Zone complete with Woody Woodpecker's

(continued on next page)

Nuthouse Coaster, Fievel's Playland (ready to walk through a huge boot—you see the world from mouse eyes!), and a playground called Curious George Goes to Town, with spray guns and buckets that dump water on visitors from above.

Everyone will love Universal Studios' newest attraction—Despicable Me Minion Mayhem—a 3-D adventure with the characters from the hit movie. Show off your dance moves!

A LOCAL KID SAYS:
"I dump water on my head when I'm really hot."
—Alex, 11, Orlando

A LOCAL KID SAYS:
"Go to inside attractions when it rains."
—Hunter, 10, Orlando

Find and circle the hidden words!

Butterbeer	Owl
Dragon	Quidditch
Gryffindor	Triwizard
Hogsmeade	Wand
Hogwarts	

```
D  V  U  B  R  P  Z  T  H  R  N  P  H
R  W  P  G  J  P  B  E  E  C  E  J  O
A  B  W  G  R  O  H  E  M  E  O  A  G
G  N  A  N  L  Y  B  E  M  R  W  R  S
O  X  N  E  D  R  F  O  A  E  L  I  M
N  E  D  O  E  I  Q  F  P  R  N  A  E
U  T  D  T  N  F  H  J  I  H  W  T  A
G  B  T  L  L  F  O  N  G  N  H  O  D
Q  U  I  D  D  I  T  C  H  R  D  R  E
B  I  A  T  T  A  R  X  T  M  Q  O  C
Y  O  N  M  C  I  S  E  R  E  F  A  R
H  O  G  W  A  R  T  S  W  E  H  E  H
F  F  Z  T  R  I  W  I  Z  A  R  D  Z
```

See page 130 for the answers!

7
SeaWorld

Want to get wet?

Head to SeaWorld's famous **Splash Zone** at Shamu Stadium. You're guaranteed to get soaked as the Shamu family of whales, including Baby Shamu, struts their stuff swimming and leaping. Watch the older whales teaching the younger ones!

{ What's Cool? To find out more about SeaWorld's animals, visit seaworld.org.

DID YOU KNOW?

Dolphins live in groups called pods. At sea, bottlenose dolphins chase one another, toss seaweed, jump, and "surf" ocean swells. Sometimes they ride the bow and stern wakes at either ends of boats. At SeaWorld, bottlenose dolphins perform in the dolphin show, where they jump, splash, and interact with each other and their trainers.

SeaWorld is the place to get up close to whales, dolphins (check out the **Dolphin Cove** and **Dolphin Nursery**), and sea lions (everybody thinks they're really funny at the **Clyde and Seamore Take Pirate Island Show**), and at **Pacific Point Preserve,** you'll hear the sea lions and harbor seals making a racket. Look at poisonous fish and a tank with six species of sharks at the **Shark Encounter.** They swim over and under you as you walk through a clear tunnel. Birds join the whales and dolphins at the **Blue Horizons** show at the Whale and Dolphin theater, while dogs and cats take to the stage at **Pets Ahoy!** (Bet your pooch can't do these kinds of tricks!)

TurtleTrek is a one-of-a-kind attraction that shows you the journey of a sea turtle through a 3-D environment that isn't only in front of you but all around you. Besides the turtle, you'll meet all kinds of sea creatures here. There are two huge saltwater and freshwater habitats, home to sea turtles that were rescued, manatees, and all kinds of fish.

DID YOU KNOW?

Male killer whales grow to be 32 feet long and weigh 8,000 to 12,000 pounds. Adult females are smaller—about 18 feet long and weighing 3,000 to 8,000 pounds.

Do you like coasters? Then you are in luck at SeaWorld Orlando. **Kraken** (named after the underwater beast from mythology) doesn't have a floor—you're in open-sided seats with your feet dangling! There's also **Journey to Atlantis,** which takes you down a 60-foot waterfall, and Manta, a steel coaster where you lie facedown underneath a giant manta ray. There are rolls, drops, and plenty of thrills for those at least 54 inches tall.

Maybe you'd prefer to kiss a dolphin. SeaWorld has that covered too at **Discovery Cove,** just across the street from SeaWorld Orlando. It lets you get up close and personal with a dolphin in the water (you only

A VISITING KID SAYS:
"There aren't as many rides at SeaWorld, but the animals make up for it."
—Noah, 12, Jacksonville, FL

have to be six!), hand-feed tropical birds in their aviary, and snorkel among thousands of colorful fish and rays in the **Grand Reef.** There's **Freshwater Oasis** that lets you get face-to-face with Asian small-clawed otters (some of them are only 2 pounds!) and check out the marmoset monkeys jumping from tree to tree. Can you hear them whistle?

Discovery Cove is all lagoons, tropical reefs, winding rivers, and beaches. There are 10,000 tropical fish and more than 250 exotic birds. Check out the Grand Reef! If you are a good swimmer, you can sign on for **SeaVenture,** an underwater walking tour—you've got a dive helmet on so you can get really close to some of the fish and sharks (don't worry, they're behind huge windows). You don't have to worry about it getting too crowded because only about 1,000 people are admitted each day and everyone gets to do everything for the one entry fee.

DID YOU KNOW?

Sea lion colonies are noisy places because sea lions often call loudly to each other. You can hear them bark and see them swim, dive, and jump at the funny sea lion and otter show at SeaWorld.

If waterslides are more your speed, SeaWorld's **Aquatica** water park, also across the street from SeaWorld Orlando, has got huge waterslides—everything from the Omaka Rocka that's almost vertical to the superfast Roa's Rapids to the eight-lane Taumata Racer. You'll fly down six stories on HooRoo Run or catch a wave in Big Surf Shores.

If you'd rather just play in the water, head to Kata's Kookaburra Cove with fountains and gentler rides and slides. Float around Loggerhead Lane on the lazy river where you can see Commerson's dolphins, colorful birds, and fish.

How many fish can you name?

{ What's Cool? There is an entire area of the SeaWorld website just for kids (seaworld.org/fun-zone/index.htm).

A VISITING KID SAYS:
"Keep your eyes on the dolphins because they are really funny. I like SeaWorld the best of the parks because of all the animals and the entertainment!"
—Morgan, 10, Chicago, IL

DID YOU KNOW?
Gray whales migrate each winter from the Arctic to Baja California, Mexico, and back: about 6,500 miles each way. The journey takes about 56 days.

76

TELL THE ADULTS:

- You can meet the Shamu character and others at **Shamu's Party Zone** during seasonal events such as the **Halloween Spooktacular** and **Just For Kids** located at Lakeside Patio, where kids can sing, dance, and party with a DJ spinning the latest music. Check when you can have Breakfast with Elmo and Friends at the Seafire Inn. Make reservations at (888) 800-5447.

A LOCAL KID SAYS:
"Every kid should go home with a stuffed animal from one of the theme parks."
—Lindsey, 12, Orlando

- You can have a sleepover at SeaWorld and dream next to either manatees, dolphins, beluga whales, polar bears, and penguins or coral reefs (seaworld .org/adventure-camps/swf/sleepover/index.htm). There are also many different behind-the-scenes tours where you can talk to animal keepers.

- Buy tickets online to save time. There are many deals that combine SeaWorld tickets with those for Busch Gardens (seaworldgetaways.com). Book in advance if you plan to go to Discovery Cove and swim with the dolphins (you have to be at least six) as only 1,000 people are admitted each day.

Helping Endangered Animals

Calling something an endangered species means this animal or plant is in danger of disappearing completely from our planet. The Florida manatee is one of the most endangered marine mammals in the United States. Each year, many Florida manatees are killed and injured by boats, the greatest human-induced cause of Florida manatee deaths. You can meet rescued West Indian manatees at the new TurtleTrek at SeaWorld Orlando.

Many other species are threatened, which means that unless conservation efforts are started, they're likely to become endangered.

SeaWorld helps endangered and protected species like Florida manatees through a rescue and rehabilitation program. Marine mammals that are sick, hurt, or orphaned as babies are brought to SeaWorld where veterinarians and other animal care specialists treat them. Sea turtles, sea otters, and manatees are some of the animals rescued by SeaWorld in San Antonio, San Diego, and Orlando. It's been 45 years since SeaWorld's rescue programs started, and more than 20,000 animals have been rescued and, in most instances, returned to the wild. SeaWorld Orlando has rehabilitated and released hundreds of manatees and returned more than 1,300 sea turtles back to their waters. Those at the TurtleTrek that can't be released because of illness or being orphaned too young to understand how to survive in the wild can live happily here.

What You Can Do to Help Our Planet

Animals and humans are part of one world with one ocean that it is up to us to protect. Every day, you can do small, simple things to help:

Turn off lights when you leave a room. Turn off the television if no one is watching it.

Create a recycling center in your home and recycle newspapers, glass, and aluminum cans.

Turn off the water while brushing your teeth.

Use both sides of a piece of paper.

Plant wildflowers in your garden instead of picking them out in nature.

Reduce the amount of trash you create: Reuse your lunch bag each day.

Don't buy animals or plants taken illegally from the wild. Ask where they're from.

Share what you know with family and friends.

DID YOU KNOW?

Sea turtles return to the beach where they were hatched to lay their own eggs. You can learn all about them at SeaWorld Orlando's TurtleTrek, where manatees and fish also live in huge saltwater and freshwater habitats.

Names for the Water "Tricks"

Bow: A leap out of the water by an animal such as a dolphin, penguin, or sea lion.

Breach: When a whale, dolphin, or sea lion jumps out of the water and lands on its side or back.

Lobtail: When the animals slap the tail flukes on the surface of the water (flukes are the horizontal lobes of the tail of a whale, dolphin, or porpoise, made of connective tissue, not bone).

Spyhop: To rise vertically out of the water so that the eye is above the surface.

DID YOU KNOW?

The most critical aspect of training an animal like Shamu to entertain guests is building a strong relationship between trainer and animal. One of the most common rewards trainers use is food. But to keep training sessions interesting and rewarding for the animals, SeaWorld trainers use a variety of different reinforcers—stroking their skin or fur and giving them squirts from the water hose, chunks of ice, and lots of positive attention.

KNOW YOUR SEA ANIMALS

Match these sea animals to their traits.

____ Beluga Whale   ____ Green Sea Turtle

____ Manatees   ____ Manta Ray

____ Asian Small-Clawed Otter

A) This animal is closely related to sharks. It has a skeleton made out of cartilage instead of bone. It also loves to swim along the bottom of the ocean, sucking up its food from the mud. It can crush the hard shells of shellfish with its rows of flat teeth.

B) This animal is endangered. It is a reptile and can stay underwater for up to 5 hours. Some swim 1,300 miles during their migration, but they still return to the same beach every year to lay their eggs.

C) This animal is a mammal that looks like it is always smiling. It swims around under the very thick ice of the Arctic and is the color white so that it can camouflage into its surroundings.

D) This animal is an endangered marine mammal. Many of these are hurt each year by boat strikes. It loves to eat plants and can eat up to 200 pounds of food a day!

E) This animal lives in the fresh and brackish waters of Southeast Asia. It only weighs 2 to 11 pounds, and is very cute. It uses scent as its main form of communication with the others of its species—always marking and protecting its territory.

See page 130 for the answers!

8

LEGOLAND

Ready to make something happen?

Not only are you guaranteed to see something new every time you walk through LEGOLAND Florida, but you can also make things happen at each of the rides and attractions.

Think racing LEGO brick cars at the Daytona International Speedway, building a LEGO car you can test on a digitally themed track in the **Imagination Zone,** or constructing a LEGO Mindstorms robot. On the LEGO Technic Test Track Coaster, you race a life-size LEGO Technic vehicle along the track.

A VISITING KID SAYS:
"At Miniland you can see stuff you never saw before. You are never too old for LEGOLAND."
—Zach, 11, North Augusta, SC

There are 10 different zones, some designed for kids as young as two and others for middle schoolers. There's a carousel with LEGO horses and 3-D movies in **Fun Town.** You'll have fun on the **Dragon Coaster,** where you go behind the scenes at the Enchanted Castle. Watch out for the fire-breathing dragon!

{ **What's Cool?** You can play and test the latest LEGO video games at Warner Brothers Game Zone within the park's Imagination Zone.

Meet a full-size LEGO brick dinosaur on **Coastersaurus**. Parents and grandparents who visited Cypress Gardens as kids may remember the wooden coaster as the Triple Hurricane.

Even preschoolers can make things happen. They can captain their own mini boats and drive cars while you compete with them and your parents in firefighting and police vehicles to put out a "fire" or catch "robbers" at the **LEGO City Rescue Academy.** They can join the Junior Fire Brigade and extinguish "flames," get up close and personal with DUPLO farm animals, and take over a mini town built just for them.

There's even an **AQUAZONE Wave Racers** ride where you can zip in and out of waves while dodging kid-powered water blasters.

A VISITING KID SAYS:
"Make your own LEGO character at LEGOLAND. That's fun!"
—Dylan, 8, Ontario, Canada

Ride through the Safari Trek where a life-size LEGO lion will roar, an elephant will spray water, and a hippo will open his mouth wide.

At **Pirates Cove,** there's a live-action water stunt show. This is also where you'll find beautiful gardens—a great place to take a picture!

Ready to walk down the Las Vegas Strip? Of course everything is made out of LEGOS in **Miniland USA.** Tiny LEGO Kids fish from the

A VISITING KID SAYS:
"I love that LEGO Friends are for girls and there's a store at LEGOLAND Florida that sells just them."
—Carlie, 11, Fort Meyers, FL

A LOCAL KID SAYS:
"I love Wave Runners at LEGOLAND."
—Piper, 12, Orlando

Pensacola Beach Gulf Pier while adults sun themselves in South Beach, including one who is bright red from too much sun. There are seagulls and crabs, beach bikes and minigolf, a historic Florida fort, Miami's Little Havana and the State Capitol in Tallahassee, the Daytona International Speedway, the Kennedy Space Center, and even a mermaid.

Watch the yellow taxis navigate Times Square or survey San Francisco's famous Golden Gate Bridge. The biggest crowd-pleaser is the pirate village (yes, there is a battle going on, complete with some poor fellows who've already fallen prey to the hangman's noose).

What's your favorite LEGO creation?

{ **What's Cool?** You can see the White House in LEGOLAND all made of LEGO bricks. At Miniland you can visit Las Vegas, Washington DC, New York City, California, and a section all of pirates!

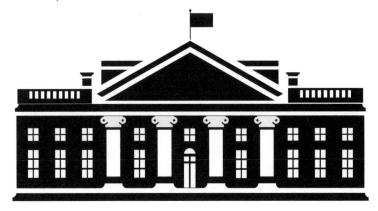

TELL THE ADULTS:

- LEGOLAND Florida is in Winter Haven, 45 minutes southwest of Orlando and 45 minutes from downtown Tampa. The address is One Legoland Way, Winter Haven, FL 33884. You can add the water park to your ticket for just $12 a person.

- There are seven educational programs incorporating science, technology, and math that meet Florida's Next Generation Sunshine State Standards. This is one theme park where kids can really learn a lot!

A LOCAL KID SAYS:
"Keep cool at a theme park when it's hot by going on water rides and eating ice cream!"
—Olivia, 13, Orlando

DID YOU KNOW?

LEGOLAND Florida is the second LEGOLAND park in the United States (the other one is in California) and the largest in the world.

Eating Smart

Do you know what foods grow in Florida? Strawberries and oranges and all kinds of vegetables.

Have you ever been to a farm? At LEGOLAND Florida's new Fresh From Florida Greenhouse, you can see Florida fruit and veggies growing and see how they're harvested and eventually make their way to your plate!

Vacations are a good time to try different foods than just what is on a kids' menu. Here at LEGOLAND you can get fresh fruit, salads, and stir-fry dishes, or even try roasted salmon—all for under $10—instead of just ordering chicken fingers and fries:

- Split a portion of something else with your brother or sister, your mom or dad.

- If there is something you like on the grown-up menu, ask if you can get a half portion or order an appetizer size.

- Opt for fruit as a snack instead of chips or candy.

- Drink water rather than a soda.

Just Add Water

LEGOLAND's new Water Park has a wave pool, Build-A-Raft lazy river where you design and build your own LEGO Vessel, tube slides, body slides, and a big interactive water-play structure.

There's plenty for littler kids too at the DUPLO Splash Safari. There are giant DUPLO creatures everywhere!

Check out Twin Chasers—tubes you ride down side by side in an enclosed space. Splash Out is the tallest point of the water park, and you can choose three different slides here and speed down a 60-foot drop. Joker Soaker has got all kinds of slides—watch out for the 300-gallon bucket that can dump on you!

How'd your raft turn out? You can try it out on the long lazy river.

A LOCAL KID SAYS:
"Mindstorms is my favorite thing at LEGOLAND."
—Jared, 11, Orlando

DID YOU KNOW?
Fifty million LEGO bricks were used to develop the park.

LEGOLAND WORD SCRAMBLE

Unscramble the names of different places you can find
built out of LEGOS at Miniland USA.

thwie ushoe

_ _ _ _ _ _ _ _ _

sla sevag

_ _ _ _ _ _ _ _

aripte galevil

_ _ _ _ _ _ _ _ _ _ _ _

stmie qraseu

_ _ _ _ _ _ _ _ _ _ _

dolgen taeg edribg

_ _ _ _ _ _ _ _ _ _ _ _ _ _ _

nnekdye capes tencer

_ _ _ _ _ _ _ _ _ _ _ _ _ _ _ _ _

tlelit nvaaha

_ _ _ _ _ _ _ _ _ _ _

tuohs cbaeh

_ _ _ _ _ _ _ _ _

See page 131 for the answers!

9
There's More to Orlando
than Theme Parks

Take your pick—minigolf, go-karts, shopping, magic shows,

a dinner with knights . . . even the chance to go up in a hot air balloon or skydiving.

At least you'll feel like you are skydiving at iFly Orlando (6805 Visitor Dr.; 407-903-1150 or 800-759-3861; iflyorlando.com), which puts you in a giant wind tunnel where you float around.

There's as much to do outside Orlando's theme parks as in them and that goes for restaurants too. You can find every kind of food here from fast food and pizza to Chinese and sushi, Italian and Mexican, even African.

A VISITING KID SAYS:

"The parks are really different. I go to different ones for different reasons. Magic Kingdom is all about the princesses and characters. Hollywood Studios is how to make movies. Animal Kingdom has animals, and Epcot is cultural."
—Alicia, 11, Alexandria, VA

{ **What's Cool?** DisneyQuest at Downtown Disney is 5 floors packed with video games, including one in which you create your own coaster at CyberSpace Mountain and ride on it in a simulator. It's a great bet when the weather is nasty!

If you're staying at a rental house or condo, maybe you'll want to go to the Orlando Farmer's Market (Lake Eola Park on the corner of E. Central Boulevard and N. Eola Drive; orlandofarmers market.com) and buy fixings for dinner.

If you are staying at a hotel within Walt Disney World or Universal Studios Orlando, you may want to try a restaurant at one of the other resorts. At Animal Kingdom Lodge, you can try food from Africa while you watch giraffes, zebras, and other animals that live right near the

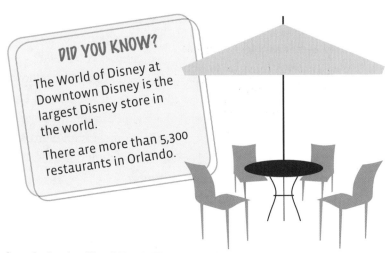

hotel. At the Hard Rock Hotel at Universal Orlando, you might see a rock star doing a cooking demonstration at The Kitchen restaurant.

Who gets to pick what kind of food your family eats on vacation?

There are also a lot of dinner shows like the **Medieval Times Dinner and Tournament** (4510 W. Vine St., Kissimmee; 866-543-9637; medievaltimes.com/Orlando. aspx) where you eat while knights perform stunts and compete against each other. At the **Outta Control Magic Show at WonderWorks** (9067 International Dr., Orlando; 407-351-8800; wonderworksonline.com), magicians perform while you eat pizza. Maybe you'll get called onstage!

{ **What's Cool?** There are more than a dozen minigolf courses in and around Orlando.

Local kids like **Fun Spot Action Park** (5551 Del Verde Way, Orlando; 407-363-3867; funspot.tutengraphics.com)—you can see it from I-Drive because of its giant Ferris wheel. Here's a place that the locals say has got some of the best go-kart tracks around (you've got to be at least 8 and 50 inches tall to ride the shortest of the four tracks) as well as bumper cars and bumper boats. There's also the **Magical Midway** (7001 International Dr.; 407-370-5353; magicalmidway.com).

Everyone who likes sports likes the **ESPN Wide World of Sports Complex** (700 S. Victory Way, Kissimmee; espnwwos.disney.go.com). It's huge! Not only is there a baseball field, but you could see basketball, wrestling, volleyball, track and field, tennis, football, and more. There's even a Playstation Pavilion.

What's your favorite sport?

What's Cool? DisneyQuest at Downtown Disney is 5 floors packed with video games, including one in which you create your own coaster at CyberSpace Mountain and ride on it in a simulator. It's a great bet when the weather is nasty!

A LOCAL KID SAYS:
"Always have sunscreen in your pocket!"
—Lindsey, 12, Orlando

TELL THE ADULTS:

- The Crossroad of Lake Buena Vista shopping center, near the hotels on Hotel Plaza Boulevard and on FL 535, has a Gooding's supermarket that's open 24 hours.

- The pools at Disney World hotels stay open 24 hours so you can go for a swim after you've watched the evening fireworks. And some of the pools are just like a water park with slides, water cannons, and kids' play areas.

A VISITING KID SAYS:
"I decide ahead of time which rides I wanted to go on with my mom and with my dad."
—Elsa, 8, Chicago, IL

A LOCAL KID SAYS:
"When it's hot, buy a fan from a souvenir truck!"
—Caroline, 10, Orlando

Souvenir Smarts

Mickey Mouse ears, a stuffed Shamu, or a blue Cat in the Hat wig ...

Whatever you don't want to leave Orlando without, you are bound to find here. Let's not forget there are many outlet stores and 12 shopping malls! (Visitorlando.com can tell you exactly where they are!)

But shop smart! That means talking to your parents about exactly how much you may spend. Save your pennies and quarters before you come. Some families save loose change in a jar to use for Orlando souvenirs. Got any birthday money you can add?

Do you want to use your money for one *big* souvenir (a stuffed Mickey or a pricey sweatshirt)? Or several smaller ones? Do you want a special T-shirt from a particular attraction or with your favorite character?

Resist those impulse buys (each attraction likely will tempt you with everything from T-shirts to swords). Wait until the end of the day or the end of the trip to shop. After a few days, you'll have a better idea of what you really can't leave without!

Think about choosing something you could only get in Orlando. Start a collection! You can buy stickers to put on your reusable water bottle. You can collect pins—as is so popular here—or patches to put on your backpack.

What else could you collect?

Downtown Disney, CityWalk & Boardwalk

A lot of local kids like Downtown Disney and CityWalk at Universal Orlando because it's fun to walk around, shop, and watch the action—and it doesn't cost anything just to be there! Check out the LEGO Imagination Center at Downtown Disney where you can make your own LEGO masterpiece.

It's also fun to take a stroll on Disney's Boardwalk where there are classic carnival games, street entertainers, restaurants, and more. You can sing along at Jellyrolls or watch your favorite athletes on TV at the ESPN Zone. Rent a bike built for four! The Boardwalk is near Epcot and Disney's Hollywood Studios.

Of course you can spend plenty here too. All three locations have lots of restaurants, shopping, and entertainment. Get your face painted or go to the movies—the AMC Complex at Universal has 20 theaters! You can even go hot air ballooning at Downtown Disney West Side.

DID YOU KNOW?

An airboat is a flat-bottomed boat that can travel on both water and flat land. It's a great way to explore the wetlands around Orlando and the creatures that live there. You'll likely see an alligator and a bald eagle!

Take in a show. At Downtown Disney you can go see Cirque du Soleil—performed in a giant circus tent with acrobats, gymnasts, and dancers all wearing amazing costumes (you can get tickets at disneyworld.com/cirque or 407-939-7600)—rent a boat, or shop till you drop. Check out the water fountains at the Marketplace. Some of them look like Mickey Mouse.

At Universal Orlando, you'll love the Blue Man Group—even though the three performers are blue, bald, and don't talk. They're going to make fun of everyone's obsession with technology. Think gigantic iPads! You'll love the drums and mystery goo! You can buy tickets at universalorlando.com/blueman.

Like hoops? At CityWalk, you can go to NBA City where you can watch NBA games while you eat. On the Boardwalk, there's the ESPN Club that's got more than 100 TVs showing live sports events.

DID YOU KNOW?

There are so many hotel rooms at Walt Disney World that you could stay in a different one each night for almost 70 years. Make sure to ask for a wake-up call if you're staying at one because Mickey Mouse might be calling!

Holidays

Christmas lasts a lot longer than just one day in Orlando. It lasts a whole month!

Have you ever seen a 30-foot-tall Christmas tree made of LEGO bricks? Here's your chance at **LEGOLAND Florida's Christmas Bricktacular.** You can find Santa in the park's botanical gardens.

Walt Disney World's got **Mickey's Very Merry Christmas Party** at the Magic Kingdom, The Osborne Family Spectacle of Dancing Lights at Disney's Hollywood Studios, and Holidays Around the World at Epcot. There's also a Christmas parade complete with Santa and a magical snowfall.

Don't miss the **Christmas Celebration at SeaWorld** with a Winter Wonderland ice-skating show, special nighttime Shamu show, live theatrical performances, and more.

At Universal Orlando Resort, Seuss Landing at Islands of Adventure is transformed for **Grinchmas** with a live show featuring who else but the Grinch! The Macy's Holiday Parade features spectacular floats, marching bands, and festive music.

Light Up UCF turns Orlando's largest university into a winter wonderland with ice-skating, treats, and even rides (want to go on the Santa train?), while the Festival of Trees at the Orlando Museum of Art features not only beautiful Christmas trees but a Gingerbread Village and Toyland Town.

Want to visit an ice park? It's at **ICE!** at the Gaylord Palms Resort (gaylordhotels.com). Check out the huge ice slides and sculptures all made out of ice.

For more information on these events go to visitorlando .com.

Kid-Friendly Orlando Restaurants

- Greek food at **Taverna Opa** off I-Drive (9101 International Dr., second floor of Pointe Orlando Plaza, Orlando, FL; 407-351-8660)

- **The Rusty Spoon** in downtown Orlando where they make their own ketchup and the food comes from local farms. Call and ask about a farm tour! (55 W. Church St., Orlando, FL; 407-401-8811)

- For pasta and really good pizza, **Cariera's Cucina Italiana** (Dr. Phillips MarketPlace, 7600 Dr. Phillips Blvd., Orlando, FL; 407-351-1187; carieras orlando.com)

- Seafood at the **Fulton Crab House** in Downtown Disney (1670 E. Buena Vista Dr., Downtown Disney, Lake Buena Vista, FL; 407-934-2628)

10

Beyond Orlando

Welcome aboard!

All those months of planning . . . that long plane ride . . . and now you're really here on a big cruise ship.

A lot of families combine a **Disney Cruise** or one on another cruise line with a visit to Orlando. You can cruise from Port Canaveral, about an hour from Orlando on Carnival Cruise Lines and Royal Caribbean International, as well as on a Disney Cruise.

Look around at all the other kids. There may be hundreds on board who want to make new friends, just like you! On Disney's ships, your favorite characters and princesses will be sailing with you too.

DID YOU KNOW?

Well over a million kids cruise each year.

A VISITING KID SAYS:
"Swimming is one of the funnest things to do on a ship. The pool is a good place to meet new friends."
—Jessica, 11, New Jersey

It seems like the whole crew—and there are a lot of them—are smiling at you as you board the ship. They're from all over the world and may not get to see their families for months at a time. Ask them to show you pictures of their kids.

You'll see a lot of people in white uniforms. They have all different jobs, from mopping the deck to serving drinks to figuring out the ship's route. The captain is the boss. You'll probably hear him on the loudspeakers making announcements.

What's Cool? Cruise ships are big, and it is easy to get lost. So kids can put pictures or decorations on the door to their staterooms (that's what rooms are called on board) to make it easier to find. Bring along some tape!

The ship is huge—more like a floating hotel or even a small town. There are restaurants and swimming pools, movie theaters and libraries, Internet cafes, musical theaters and, most important, huge Kids Clubs.

The first thing you need to do is figure out where your stateroom is. It's probably smaller than your room at home, but it's so cozy! Does your bed fold down from the wall at night? If you're lucky, you'll discover a towel-animal when you go to bed. Ask your steward—the person who takes care of your cabin—to show how to make a monkey or a duck. Some kids put a picture on their door so they know which stateroom is theirs because they all look alike.

Every night, your steward will leave you a schedule of the next day's activities—specialized for your age group—at the Kids Club. You can stay busy from morning until late at night! Take your pick: scavenger hunts, game night, dinners, karaoke, talent shows, the latest computer and arcade games. The counselors here can help you to meet some kids—especially if you're shy. The Kids Club is probably the second place you want to find on board after your stateroom. A lot of times it's on one of the top decks, near the pool. And the counselors usually have an "open house" the first afternoon or night of the cruise.

A LOCAL KID SAYS:
"My favorite thing to do in Orlando outside of theme parks is go horseback riding!"
—Natalie, 12, Orlando

There's also a lot to do with your family—shows at night, karaoke, basketball and shuffleboard, table tennis, and the hot tubs.

You'll be just as busy off the ship exploring the ports with your family. You may go to the cruise line's private island too. Fun!

{ **What's Cool?** On board ship, your meals, except at certain places, have already been paid for so you can order whatever you like—there's no extra charge—even for seconds! A cruise is a great time to try foods you may not have eaten before!

The other good news on board is you should never be hungry. There's food somewhere all day and all evening— pizza, ice cream, cookies, sandwiches, fruit . . . You can order room service for free too. Some kids like to order a snack when they get back from exploring the ports with their families.

A lot of kids like to go to the Kids Clubs just so they can hang out with their friends—and without their moms and dads. The clubs are open at night so you can eat dinner with your family and then meet up with your friends.

Even though the ship is big, you'll have it figured out in a day or so. Quick tip: A lot of times it's faster to go up and down the stairs than to wait for the elevators.

Another tip: If you're really hungry in the morning, go to the buffet where you can get a lot of different food fast.

Mickey-shaped waffles anybody?

{ **What's Cool?** The inside cabins of Disney's newest ships have "virtual portholes" where you might see your favorite characters float by.

A LOCAL KID SAYS:
"Go to the Mall at Millenia for shopping and great food!"
—Nicole, 11, Orlando

TELL THE ADULTS:

- Soon after you board ship, there will be a safety drill where you will all gather at your muster stations with your life vests—the same place you would go in an emergency. It is important to make sure everyone in your family knows how to get there and what to do if there is an emergency because kids and parents on board ship likely won't be together all the time with all the activities on board.

- If you are planning to go to SeaWorld and Busch Gardens Tampa Bay, as well as Universal Studios Orlando, consider the Orlando Flex Ticket. There are also combination tickets to SeaWorld and Busch Gardens. You'll find information on buschgardens.com and seaworld.com. At Busch Gardens, check out an up close adventure or behind-the-scenes tour like the Serengeti Safari or Elephant Keeper Experience. Take a look behind the action as a Roller Coaster Insider where you can learn how roller coasters are built.

- If you've never cruised before, it's smart to take along some over the counter medicine for motion sickness just in case. Some people think sea bands that you put on your wrists help.

The Rockets Red Glare

Kennedy Space Center (kennedyspacecenter.com—check out the page for kids!), SR 405, Kennedy Space Center, FL, 32899; (866) 737-5235.

Welcome to the launch site for most of the US space programs. This is where astronauts blasted off to the moon and on shuttle missions. Today, though there are currently no manned-spaceflight launches, you can visit, meet, and even have lunch with an astronaut. It's less than an hour's drive from Orlando and well worth the trip.

See what is happening at the *International Space Station* when you visit the Launch Status Center. There's a children's play dome, IMAX movies, and all kinds of exhibits of everything from space suits to lunar landers and capsules.

You can take a bus around the Kennedy Space Center and stop at different exhibits for as long as you like. Don't miss the Apollo/*Saturn V* Center that is built around the 363-foot *Saturn V* moon rocket. You can time travel back to 1968 for the launch of the first manned mission to the moon. See the countdown clocks and launch controls.

You'll like the hands-on Exploration Space: Explorers Wanted exhibit that raises questions like where we might go next in space or how spacecraft will work in the future. Check out the Rocket Garden with all kinds of rockets and spacecraft.

Ready to blast off?

Safaris & Coasters

Welcome to Africa—Florida style. **Busch Gardens Tampa Bay** (10165 N. McKinley Dr., Tampa, FL; buschgardens.com; 888-800-5447), about a 90-minute drive from Orlando, is divided into nine African regions.

Many families come here because of Busch Gardens' huge coasters. There are six of them! As long as you're 48 inches tall, go to Gwazi, the double wooden coaster, first thing to avoid long lines. You have to be 54 inches tall and love intense rides for Montu, the inverted steel coaster where your feet dangle in the air. Get soaked on the Congo River Rapids and Tanganyika Tidal Wave. If you're not tall enough for them, go with a grown-up on the Stanley Falls Flume.

There's also plenty for those who don't like or are too small for scary coasters. At the Animal Care Center you can watch the park's veterinarians take care of the animals—maybe even see a surgery. You could have the chance to help prepare the food for the animals.

Ready to "cook" with crickets?

A LOCAL KID SAYS:
"I love coasters! How can you live in Orlando and not?"
—Mary, 13, Orlando

TILE SCRAMBLE

Try to unscramble the tiles and figure out the sentence!

| OUTSIDE | IS | SO | ORLANDO! |

| THERE | OF | TO | MUCH |

| DO |

See page 131 for the answer!

DID YOU KNOW?

Astronauts from different countries spend months at a time living and working far above the earth at the International Space Station.

What a Trip!

I came to Orlando on:

_____

_____

_____

We stayed ___ days.

_____

_____

_____

I came to Orlando with:

_____

_____

_____

The weather was:

_____

_____

_____

We went to:

_____

_____

_____

We ate:

_____

_____

_____

We bought:

_____

_____

_____

I saw these famous Orlando sites:

_____

_____

_____

My favorite thing about Orlando was:

_____

_____

_____

My best memory of Orlando was:

_____

_____

_____

These are the characters I saw:

_____

_____

_____

_____

_____

_____

My favorite amusement park ride was:

_____

_____

_____

_____

_____

My favorite souvenir is:

_____

_____

_____

_____

_____

You have had such a great time in Orlando! Draw some pictures or paste in some photos of your trip!

Index

Answer Keys

Magic Kingdom Crossword Puzzle (pp. 24–25)

Across

1) Snow White

2) Space Mountain

3) Missouri

4) FASTPASS

5) Imagineers

Down

1) Swiss Family Robinson

6) Tomorrowland

7) Adventureland

8) Fairytale Hall

9) Haunted Mansion

Living with the Land (p. 35)

Answers:

Root–Carrot

Stem–Asparagus

Leaves–Lettuce

Flower–Broccoli

Fruit–Tomato

Seed–Sunflower Seeds

Answer: The four things that all plants need to survive are Sun, Soil, Water, and Air

What did you learn about Disney's Animal Kingdom? (p. 45)

Answers:

1) Komodo Dragon

2) Kilimanjaro

3) Paleontologist

4) Zebra

5) Simba

6) Anemone

7) Grasshopper

Secret Word: Amazing

Word Puzzle (p. 55)

Answer: Honey, I Shrunk the Kids!

Harry Potter Word Search (p. 69)

D	V	U	B	R	P	Z	T	H	**R**	N	P	**H**
R	W	P	**G**	J	P	B	E	**E**	C	E	J	**O**
A	B	**W**	G	**R**	O	H	**E**	M	E	**O**	A	**G**
G	N	**A**	N	L	**Y**	**B**	E	M	R	**W**	R	**S**
O	X	**N**	E	D	**R**	**F**	O	A	E	**L**	I	**M**
N	E	**D**	O	**E**	I	Q	**F**	P	R	N	A	**E**
U	T	D	**T**	N	F	H	J	**I**	H	W	T	**A**
G	B	**T**	L	L	F	O	N	G	**N**	H	O	**D**
Q	**U**	**I**	**D**	**D**	**I**	**T**	**C**	**H**	R	**D**	R	**E**
B	I	A	T	T	A	R	X	T	M	Q	**O**	C
Y	O	N	M	C	I	S	E	R	E	F	A	**R**
H	**O**	**G**	**W**	**A**	**R**	**T**	**S**	W	E	H	E	H
F	F	Z	**T**	**R**	**I**	**W**	**I**	**Z**	**A**	**R**	**D**	Z

Know Your Sea Animals (p. 81)

Answers:

C   Beluga Whale

E   Asian Small-Clawed Otter

B   Green Sea Turtle

D   Manatees

A   Manta Ray

LEGOLAND Word Scramble (p. 91)

Answers:

1) White House

2) Las Vegas

3) Pirate Village

4) Times Square

5) Golden Gate Bridge

6) Kennedy Space Center

7) Little Havana

8) South Beach

Tile Scramble (p. 114)

Answer: There is so much to do outside of Orlando!

About the Author

Award-winning author Eileen Ogintz is a leading national family travel expert whose syndicated "Taking the Kids" is the most widely distributed column in the country on family travel. She has also created TakingtheKids.com, which helps families make the most of their vacations together. Ogintz is the author of seven family travel books and is often quoted in major publications such as *USA Today*, the *Wall Street Journal*, and the *New York Times*, as well as parenting and women's magazines on family travel. She has appeared on such television programs as *The Today Show*, *Good Morning America*, and *The Oprah Winfrey Show*, as well as dozens of local radio and television news programs. She has traveled around the world with her three children and others in the family, talking to other traveling families wherever she goes. She is also the author of *The Kid's Guide to New York City* (Globe Pequot Press).